SUCCESS WITH C

SUCCESS WITH
CANAPES

INVADER

AUBERGINE MOUSSE

1 small aubergine olive oil
1 shallot, chopped
1 clove garlic
1 oz (25 g) grated coconut
1 tbsp (1x15 ml spoon)
  tomato ketchup
1 tsp (1x5 ml spoon)
` ground ginger
salt
cayenne pepper
2 tbsps (2x15 ml spoons)
  soft white cheese
10 thin toast triangles
stuffed olives, cut into
  thin circles
parsley

For ten canapés

1 Coat the aubergine with oil and put under a hot grill until the skin begins to wrinkle.
2 To make the mousse, remove skin from aubergine and purée the flesh in a blender, adding grated coconut and shallot.
3 Season with ginger, salt and cayenne pepper.
4 Stir in cheese and ketchup.
5 Cut clove of garlic in half, rub the toast triangles with garlic and spread the mousse on to them.
6 Garnish with circles of stuffed olive and sprigs of parsley.

OLIVE BUTTER SNACKS

4 oz (100 g) butter
4 oz (100 g) Gorgonzola
  cheese
1 tbsp (1x15 ml spoon)
  grappa (Italian liqueur)
10 green olives, stoned
  and finely chopped
10 small crisp toast circles
1 tomato
fresh basil leaves

For ten canapés

1 Mix cheese and butter together until smooth, then add the olives.
2 Stir in grappa.
3 Put mixture in the refrigerator until firm.
4 Use a piping bag to pipe rosettes of mixture on to the toasts.
5 Garnish with small pieces of tomato and basil leaves.

ANCHOVIES ON RYE BREAD

10 thin circles rye bread
2 tbsps (2x15 ml spoons)
  mayonnaise
3 tomatoes, sliced thinly
1 courgette, sliced
sprigs of fresh dill
10 anchovy fillets
½ red pepper

For ten canapés

1 Spread mayonnaise on to bread circles.
2 Cover each circle with a slice of tomato, a slice of courgette, a sprig of dill, and a rolled anchovy fillet.
3 Garnish with small pieces of red pepper.

TOAST CANAPES

AUBERGINE MOUSSE
OLIVE BUTTER SNACKS
ANCHOVIES ON RYE BREAD

ANCHOVY TRIANGLES

1 can anchovy fillets
3 cloves garlic
1 tbsp (1x15 ml spoon)
  capers
4 oz (100 g) soft white
  cheese
juice of ½ lemon
10 thin toast triangles
1 tomato
chives

For ten canapés
1 Drain the anchovies.
2 Peel garlic cloves and blanch in boiling water for 2 minutes.
3 Blend cheese, lemon juice, anchovies and garlic.
4 Stir in capers and spread paste on to the toast triangles.
5 Garnish each canapé with a piece of tomato and chives.

SALMON BOATS

12 oz (300 g) smoked
  salmon, thinly sliced
cognac
pepper
salt
3½ fl oz (100 ml) crème
  fraîche
10 small toast ovals
fresh parsley

For ten boats
1 Put 1 slice of salmon aside for garnish. Put the rest in a blender together with a dash of cognac, pepper and salt, and purée.
2 Put the mixture in the refrigerator to chill.
3 Meanwhile, whip the crème fraîche. Stir in the salmon paste.
4 Put back in refrigerator until firm.
5 Pile salmon mousse on to toasts. Garnish with parsley and thin strips of salmon.

HERRING CANAPES

¼ celeriac
juice of ¼ lemon
2 tbsps (2x15 ml spoons)
  mayonnaise
1 tsp (1x5 ml spoon)
  mustard
pepper
10 small toast circles
2-3 matjes (young herring,
  salted)
cress
1 red pepper

For ten canapés
1 Coarsely grate celeriac and stir in lemon juice, mayonnaise and mustard. Season with pepper.
2 Pile mixture on to the toasts. Cut matjes into small pieces and place a piece on each toast.
3 Make small circle shapes from red pepper and use these and cress for garnish.

ANCHOVY TRIANGLES
SALMON BOATS
HERRING CANAPES

9

SCAMPI ALFALFA
FILET AMERICAIN WITH CAPERS
MASCARPONE WITH RADISHES

QUAIL'S EGGS WITH CAVIAR
HAM AND MANGO CHUTNEY CANAPES
LIVER PATE CRACKERS

4 oz (100 g) Mascarpone
 (white Italian cheese)
pepper
salt
1 shallot, finely chopped
10 crisp toast circles
5 small radishes, sliced

MASCARPONE WITH RADISHES

For ten canapés

1 Season cheese with pepper and salt.
2 Mix cheese and shallot, and spread on to the toasts.
3 Cut each radish slice in two and put one half aside. Place a half slice of radish upright in the middle of each canapé.
4 Cut the remaining half slices in two and add two quarters to each canapé to form a cross.

1 hen's egg, hard-boiled
1 tbsp (1x15 ml spoon)
 mustard
olive oil
pepper
salt
1 lemon
1 shallot, chopped
2-3 chives, finely chopped
10 crisp toast squares
3 fresh quail's eggs,
 hard-boiled
1 small jar caviar

QUAIL'S EGGS WITH CAVIAR

For ten canapés

1 Mash hen's egg with a fork, mix with mustard and add oil, a little at a time, to make a thick mayonnaise.
2 Season with pepper, salt and lemon juice. Add shallot and chives and spread mixture on to toast.
3 Shell quail's eggs, cut into slices and put a slice on top of each canapé.
4 Garnish with a spoonful of caviar and a small piece of lemon.

4 oz (100 g) ham
10 small squares rye toast
butter
mango chutney (medium
 hot)
lemon peel

HAM AND MANGO CHUTNEY CANAPES

For ten canapés

1 Cut ham into thin strips.
2 Butter toasts and top with rolled strips of ham.
3 Fill ham with chutney and garnish with pieces of lemon peel.

10 scampi, cooked or
   uncooked
sea salt
5 pieces wholemeal
   crispbread
2 oz (50 g) mayonnaise
1 small pot alfalfa sprouts
a sprig of fresh dill

SCAMPI ALFALFA

For ten canapés

1 If scampi are uncooked, cook in a non-stick frying pan, without adding fat, until they turn pink.
2 Sprinkle scampi with salt and add enough water to cover. Poach gently to finish cooking (4-10 minutes, depending on size).
3 Drain and shell scampi.
4 Cut crispbread in half.
5 Spread with mayonnaise and cover with alfalfa.
6 Garnish with a scampi and a small sprig of dill.

4 oz (100 g) filet
   americain (raw minced
   beefsteak)
1 egg yolk
1 shallot, finely chopped
1 tbsp (1x15 ml spoon)
   mustard
pepper
salt
Worcestershire sauce
2 tsps (2x5 ml spoons)
   capers
10 crisp toast circles

FILET AMERICAIN WITH CAPERS

For ten snacks

1 Mix filet americain and egg yolk together.
2 Add shallot, mustard, pepper, salt, Worcestershire sauce and 1 teaspoon (1x5 ml spoon) capers.
3 Pile mixture in cones on toast circles and garnish each with a caper.

4 oz (100 g) liver pâté
1 oz (30 g) soft white
   cheese
cayenne pepper
10 snack crackers
2 spring onions

LIVER PATE CRACKERS

For ten canapés

1 Mix the pâté and cheese to a smooth paste.
2 Season with cayenne pepper.
3 Put mixture into a piping bag and pipe a rosette on to each cracker.
4 Garnish with pieces of spring onion.

½ small cauliflower
salt
7 fl oz (200 ml) crème
  fraîche
10 chives, chopped
cayenne pepper
2 oz (50 g) peeled shrimps
10 bread circles
2 oz (50 g) butter, melted
sprigs of fresh chervil

CAULIFLOWER SHRIMP CANAPES

For ten canapés

1 Divide cauliflower into florets and boil in salted water.
2 Purée in a blender with crème fraîche, chives, salt, and cayenne pepper.
3 Put mixture in the refrigerator until firm.
4 Spread bread with melted butter.
5 Brown under a hot grill.
6 Put the cauliflower purée into a piping bag and pipe rosettes on to toasts. Surround with shrimps and top with chervil.

10 fresh spinach leaves
salt
1 clove garlic
2 tbsps (2x15 ml spoons)
  olive oil
10 small toast circles
1 slice feta cheese (Greek
  cheese)

SPINACH ROUNDS WITH FETA CHEESE

For ten snacks

1 Plunge the washed spinach leaves one by one into salted boiling water. Then put immediately into cold water.
2 Crush garlic in olive oil and spread on to toasts.
3 Arrange a spinach leaf in the shape of a rose on each toast and fill the centre with small pieces of cheese.

4 oz (100 g) Brussels
  cheese (sharp, soft white
  cheese)
4 oz (100 g) full fat cream
  cheese
10 toast circles
chives

CHEESE BITES WITH SESAME SEEDS

For ten canapés

1 Mix the cheeses into a cream.
2 Put into a piping bag and pipe rosettes on to toasts.
3 Brown sesame seeds in a non-stick frying pan and sprinkle over cheese.
4 Decorate with chives.

CAULIFLOWER SHRIMP CANAPES
SPINACH ROUNDS WITH FETA CHEESE
CHEESE BITES WITH SESAME SEEDS

15

3 slices smoked salmon
10 circles soft toast
3 tbsps (3x15 ml spoons)
  soft white cheese with
  herbs
1 lime

SALMON AND HERB
CHEESE CANAPES

For ten canapés
1 Cut salmon into strips and arrange in the
   shape of a rose on each toast circle.
2 Put cheese into a piping bag and pipe
   rosettes on top of salmon.
3 Garnish with a small piece of lime.

2 avocados
6 tbsps (6x15 ml spoons)
  cream cheese
2 tbsps (2x15 ml spoons)
  juice of pink grapefruit
salt
cayenne pepper
grapefruit peel
10 crisp toast circles
10 marjoram leaves

AVOCADO
CREAMS

For ten canapés
1 Cut each avocado in half.
2 Remove stone and scoop out flesh.
3 Purée flesh in a blender with cream cheese
   and grapefruit juice.
4 Season with salt, cayenne pepper and a
   little grated grapefruit peel.
5 Use a piping bag to pipe rosettes of
   avocado cream on to toasts. Garnish with
   strips of grapefruit peel and a marjoram
   leaf.

10 crisp toast circles
5 oz (150 g) Parma ham,
  thinly sliced
1 cantaloup melon
1 glass port
sprigs of fresh chervil

HAM AND MELON
SNACKS

For ten canapés
1 Cut melon in two, remove seeds and use a
   melon baller to scoop out small balls of
   fruit.
2 Marinate melon balls in the port for
   several hours.
3 Cut ham into thin strips and arrange in the
   shape of a rose on each toast circle. Put
   one melon ball into each ham rose.
4 Garnish with a sprig of chervil.

SALMON AND HERB CHEESE CANAPES
AVOCADO CREAMS
HAM AND MELON SNACKS

1 avocado
2 tbsps (2x15 ml spoons)
   cream cheese
1 tbsp (1x15 ml spoon)
   low-fat, soft white
   cheese
juice and peel of ¼ orange
pepper
salt
10 crisp toast circles

AVOCADO MOUSSE WITH ORANGE

For ten canapés

1 Peel avocado, cut in two and remove stone.
2 To make the mousse, purée avocado flesh in a blender with cheeses and orange juice.
3 Season mousse with salt and pepper, and spread on toasts.
4 Garnish with small strips of orange peel. Chill before serving.

½ avocado
juice of ¼ lemon
2 matjes fillets (young
   herring, salted)
cayenne pepper
10 small toast circles
fresh dill leaves

MATJES WITH AVOCADO

For ten canapés

1 Peel avocado and dice the flesh.
2 Immediately cover with lemon juice to prevent the flesh changing colour.
3 Dice the matjes fillets to the same size as the avocado. Mix the two together.
4 Season with cayenne pepper and put on to toasts.
5 Garnish each canapé with a small sprig of dill.

1 horseradish
10 toast circles
salt
4-5 cocktail sausages
Dijon mustard

HORSERADISH WITH COCKTAIL SAUSAGES

For ten canapés

1 Chill horseradish in the refrigerator until very crisp then peel with a sharp knife.
2 Grate horseradish and drain on kitchen paper.
3 Put strips of horseradish on toasts and sprinkle with salt.
4 Slice cocktail sausages and put two or three slices on each bed of horseradish.
5 Top with a little mustard.

18

HORSERADISH WITH COCKTAIL SAUSAGES
AVOCADO MOUSSE WITH ORANGE
MATJES WITH AVOCADO

1 x 4 oz (100 g) slice of
  garlic sausage
4 oz (100 g) Gouda cheese
10 toast squares
2 oz (50 g) butter
mustard
fresh parsley, chopped

GARLIC SAUSAGE WITH CHEESE

For ten canapés

1 Remove skin from sausage, cut into ¼ in (½ cm) slices, then dice.
2 Dice cheese to same size and mix with sausage.
3 Butter toast squares and put some diced sausage and cheese on each one.
4 Garnish with a little mustard and parsley.

4 oz (100 g) cod fillet
pepper
salt
paprika
lemon juice
1 tbsp (1x15 ml spoon)
  mayonnaise
10 snack crackers
¼ red pepper, diced
¼ green pepper, diced
10 capers

FISH AND PEPPER SALAD

For ten canapés

1 Season fish with pepper, salt and paprika. Sprinkle with lemon juice and leave for fish to absorb flavour.
2 Steam or poach until tender.
3 When fish has cooked, mash and mix with mayonnaise.
4 Spread the mixture on to crackers.
5 Put diced peppers on each canapé and garnish with a caper.

4 slices Gouda cheese
10 toast circles made from
  brown bread
2 oz (50 g) cream cheese
2 oz (50 g) Roquefort
  cheese
gin
stuffed olives, sliced

CHEESE COCKTAILS

For ten canapés

1 Cut Gouda into circles the same size as toast circles.
2 Put a circle of cheese on to each piece of toast.
3 Mix cream cheese, Roquefort and a dash of gin into a smooth paste. Use a teaspoon to spoon the mixture on to the cheese circles.
4 Put a second circle of Gouda cheese on top of mixture and press down lightly.
5 Garnish with slices of stuffed olives.

GARLIC SAUSAGE WITH CHEESE
FISH AND PEPPER SALAD
CHEESE COCKTAILS

4 oz (100 g) duck liver
  pâté
pepper
salt
nutmeg
2 oz (50 g) cream cheese
10 small crisp toast
  squares
truffle peel

DUCK LIVER PATE WITH TRUFFLES

For ten canapés

1 Season pâté with pepper, salt and nutmeg.
2 Mix cream cheese and pâté together loosely to make a two-coloured paste.
3 Put the paste into a piping bag and pipe rosettes on to toasts.
4 Chop truffle peel into small pieces.
5 Garnish with pieces of truffle peel.

1 fillet smoked trout
2-3 tbsps (2-3x15 ml
  spoons) mayonnaise
lemon juice
cayenne pepper
pinch grated horseradish
10 small toast circles
1 jar trout's eggs
fresh dill leaves

SMOKED TROUT WITH TROUT'S EGGS

For ten canapés

1 Bone the fish, mash well and mix with mayonnaise.
2 Season with lemon juice, pepper and horseradish.
3 Spread the mixture on to toasts.
4 Garnish with trout's eggs and small sprigs of dill.

2 carrots
½ horseradish
2 tbsps (2x15 ml spoons)
  mayonnaise
paprika
10 toast circles
3-4 chives, chopped

VEGETABLE CANAPES

For ten canapés

1 Peel and chop carrots and horseradish. Shred them finely in a food processor.
2 Pat vegetables dry with kitchen paper and mix with mayonnaise.
3 Season the mixture with paprika and spread on to toast circles.
4 Garnish with chopped chives.

DUCK LIVER PATE WITH TRUFFLES
SMOKED TROUT WITH TROUT'S EGGS
VEGETABLE CANAPES

4 oz (100 g) fine liver pâté
2 oz (50 g) smoked bacon
10 snack crackers
1 tomato

LIVER PATE WITH BACON

For ten canapés
1 Spread pâté on to crackers.
2 Cut bacon into small pieces and fry in its own fat in a non-stick frying pan.
3 Meanwhile, cut tomato into quarters. Remove seeds and cut the tomato into strips.
4 Put bacon on the pâté and garnish with strips of tomato.

2 beetroots, uncooked
1 tbsp (1x15 ml spoon) white vinegar
1 tbsp (1x15 ml spoon) groundnut oil
1 tbsp (1x15 ml spoon) olive oil
salt
freshly ground pepper
10 toast circles
2 small pickled herrings

MARINATED BEETROOT AND HERRING CANAPES

For ten canapés
1 Remove the beetroot tops, leaving the stem to prevent the juice escaping during cooking.
2 Cook the beetroot in their skins, without salt, for between 45 minutes and 1 hour. Peel and dice.
3 Make vinaigrette by mixing vinegar with a pinch of salt and the two oils.
4 Season with pepper.
5 Marinate diced beetroot in vinaigrette for 1 hour.
6 Put marinated beetroot on to toasts and garnish with a piece of herring.

4 oz (100 g) goat's cheese
10 small toast squares
1 pinch ground mace
red peppercorns
3-4 chives, chopped

GOAT'S CHEESE WITH PEPPERCORNS

For ten canapés
1 Spread goat's cheese on to toasts and season with ground mace.
2 Top with peppercorns and chopped chives.

MARINATED BEETROOT WITH HERRING CANAPES
GOAT'S CHEESE WITH PEPPERCORNS
LIVER PATE WITH BACON

COURGETTE CHIPS

1 lb, 2oz (500 g)
   courgettes, sliced
3 tbsps (3x15 ml spoons)
   lemon juice
flour
salt
cayenne pepper
oil for frying

For 4-6 servings

1 Cover courgette slices with lemon juice.
   Leave to absorb juice for a few minutes.
2 Coat with flour.
3 Heat some oil to 180°C/350°F and fry the
   courgette slices a few at a time.
4 Season with salt and cayenne pepper.
5 Serve hot.

STUFFED CHERRY TOMATOES

20 cherry tomatoes
salt
4 oz (100 g) feta cheese
   (Greek cheese)
2-3 tbsps (2-3x15 ml
   spoons) crème fraîche
paprika
sprigs of fresh chervil

For twenty canapés

1 Cut the tops off tomatoes and scoop out
   the insides.
2 Sprinkle insides of tomatoes with salt and
   leave upside down to drain.
3 Mix feta cheese with crème fraîche and
   pinch of paprika. Put mixture into a piping
   bag and pipe rosettes into the tomatoes.
4 Garnish with sprigs of chervil.

SOYA PARCELS

6 eggs
salt
1 tsp (1x5 ml spoon) soy
   sauce
3 tbsps (3x15 ml spoons)
   chives, chopped
cayenne pepper
spicy tomato ketchup
2 oz (50 g) soya bean
   sprouts
1 tbsp (1x15 ml spoon)
   margarine
lettuce leaves
chives

For twenty canapés

1 Beat the eggs with salt, soy sauce,
   chopped chives, cayenne pepper, and
   ketchup.
2 Fry soya bean sprouts in margarine until
   brown. Add egg mixture to make a thick
   omelette.
3 Leave omelette to cool and then dice.
4 Blanch lettuce leaves in boiling water and
   then plunge straight into cold water.
5 Wrap the diced omelette in lettuce leaves
   and tie with chives.

VEGETABLE CANAPES

STUFFED CHERRY TOMATOES
SOYA PARCELS
COURGETTE CHIPS

1 cucumber
9 oz (250 g) ham
cognac
pepper
salt
cayenne pepper
1 tsp (1x5 ml spoon)
  tomato purée
7 fl oz (200 ml) double
  cream, whipped
1 red pepper

CUCUMBER WITH HAM MOUSSE

For fifteen canapés
1 Cut cucumber into thick slices and use a melon baller or spoon to scoop a hollow in each slice. Blanch for 1 minute.
2 To make the mousse, put ham, tomato purée, pepper, salt, cayenne pepper and a dash of cognac into a blender and purée.
3 Add cream and put mixture in the refrigerator until firm.
4 Fill the cucumber slices with mousse and garnish with pieces of red pepper.

2 chicory heads
10 tsps (10x15 ml spoons)
  mayonnaise
1 tbsp (1x15 ml spoon)
  tomato ketchup
Worcestershire sauce
cayenne pepper
pepper
salt
whisky
sprig of parsley
sprig of chervil
cress
peeled prawns for garnish
stuffed olives, sliced

CHICORY CANAPES

Wash the chicory heads and cut off the base of each. Separate the leaves and lay them on a large plate. Garnish with cocktail sauce or green mayonnaise.
1 To make the cocktail sauce, mix half the mayonnaise with ketchup, a few drops of Worcestershire sauce and a dash of whisky. Season with cayenne pepper, pepper and salt.
2 To make the green mayonnaise, chop herbs finely and mix with rest of mayonnaise.
3 Pour sauces on to the chicory leaves.
4 Garnish with prawns and slices of olive.

2 large carrots
8-10 radishes
1 tbsp (1x15 ml spoon)
  raspberry vinegar
salt
1 tbsp (1x15 ml) spoon
  groundnut oil
1 tbsp (1x15 ml spoon)
  olive oil
pepper
chervil
basil leaves

RAW VEGETABLE CANAPES

For twenty canapés
1 Peel carrots and slice into rings.
2 Make a vinaigrette with vinegar, oils, salt and pepper.
3 Cut radishes into strips and marinate in vinaigrette for half an hour. Put a spoonful on to each slice of carrot and garnish with chervil and basil leaves.

CHICORY CANAPES
RAW VEGETABLE CANAPES
CUCUMBER WITH HAM MOUSSE

7 oz (200 g) Gorgonzola
  cheese
3 tbsps (3x15 ml) softened
  butter
1 bunch parsley, chopped
4 oz (100 g) walnut halves
10 medium-sized
  mushrooms

STUFFED MUSHROOMS

For ten canapés
1 Mix butter and cheese together.
2 Keep ten half walnuts for garnish. Peel
   and chop the rest finely.
3 Add chopped nuts and parsley to butter
   and cheese mixture. Put in the refrigerator
   until firm.
4 Remove stalks and wash mushrooms.
5 Put nut mixture into a piping bag and pipe
   rosettes into each mushroom hollow.
6 Garnish with half walnuts.

½ jar peeled red peppers
2 tbsps (2x15 ml spoons)
  olive oil
fresh basil leaves
2 yellow courgettes

COURGETTE AND PEPPER CANAPES

For ten canapés
1 Drain peppers and cut into strips. Keeping
   some leaves for garnish, chop basil and
   mix with olive oil. Marinate peppers in the
   oil for several hours.
2 Cut courgettes into thick slices. Use a
   melon baller or spoon to scoop out
   hollows in the flesh.
3 Fill hollows with peppers.
4 Garnish with basil leaves.

5 oz (150 g) Brie
5 oz (150 g) Danish blue
5 oz (150 g) soft white
  cheese
1 onion, finely chopped
salt
pepper
cognac
Worcestershire sauce
4-5 sticks celery

CELERY CANAPES

For fifteen canapés
1 Mix cheeses with the onion. Season with
   pepper, salt, a dash of cognac and a few
   drops of Worcestershire sauce.
2 Trim and peel celery. Cut into 2-inch
   (5 cm) pieces.
3 Put cheese mixture into a piping bag and
   pipe a strip on to each piece of celery.
   Garnish with celery leaves.

STUFFED MUSHROOMS
COURGETTE AND PEPPER CANAPES
CELERY CANAPES

4 tomatoes
1 Mozzarella cheese
1 bunch basil, chopped
pepper
salt
virgin olive oil

TOMATOES WITH MOZZARELLA

For ten servings
1 Plunge tomatoes into boiling water for 10 seconds, then peel, quarter and remove the seeds.
2 Dice the flesh.
3 Cut Mozzarella into the same number of dice.
4 Mix tomatoes, cheese and basil together. Season with pepper and salt.
5 Pour on a few drops of olive oil.

½ green pepper
½ red pepper
1 small can sweetcorn
salt
1 tbsp (1x15 ml spoon) vinegar
2 tbsps (2x15 ml spoons) olive oil
pepper
cayenne pepper
pinch sugar
pinch dried oregano
fresh parsley, chopped

SWEETCORN AND PEPPER SALAD

For ten servings
1 Wash peppers and remove seeds and core.
2 Cut into small dice.
3 Drain sweetcorn and mix with diced peppers.
4 Make vinaigrette by dissolving a pinch of salt in vinegar then whisking with oil. Season with pepper, cayenne pepper and sugar.
5 Mix vegetables with vinaigrette. Sprinkle with oregano and chopped parsley.

2 chicory heads
juice of ¼ lemon
2 tbsps (2x15 ml spoons) mayonnaise
paprika
2 oz (50 g) raisins

CHICORY AND RAISIN SALAD

For ten servings
1 Remove base and outside leaves from chicory heads and chop the rest finely.
2 Cover with lemon juice immediately to stop them going brown.
3 Add mayonnaise and raisins.
4 Season with paprika.

32

SWEETCORN AND PEPPER SALAD
CHICORY AND RAISIN SALAD
TOMATOES WITH MOZZARELLA

BUTTERNUT SQUASH CHIPS

1 butternut squash (a pear-
  shaped marrow)
salt
oil for frying

1 Peel the squash and cut into very thin slices.
2 Dry the slices on kitchen paper and then fry them in oil heated to 170°C/335°F.
3 Leave to cool and then fry for a second time at 200°C/400°F.
4 Sprinkle with salt.

CHERRY TOMATOES WITH CHEESE AND HERBS

10 cherry tomatoes
salt
1 clove garlic
2 bunches basil
1 tbsp (1x15 ml spoon) pine kernels
2 oz (50 g) Parmesan cheese, grated
olive oil

For ten tomatoes
1 Cut tops off tomatoes and scoop out the insides.
2 Sprinkle salt into tomatoes and leave them upside down to drain.
3 Peel the garlic and crush to a smooth paste with the basil leaves and a pinch salt.
4 Stir in the pine kernels and then the cheese. Lastly, add enough olive oil to make a thick paste.
5 Stuff the tomatoes with the mixture.

MUSHROOMS A LA GRECQUE

14 oz (400 g) button mushrooms
4 tbsps (4x15 ml spoons) olive oil
1 onion
pepper
salt
1 clove garlic, crushed
juice of ½ lemon
1 glass white wine
2 tbsps (2x15 ml spoons) tomato purée
parsley, chopped

For ten canapés
1 Clean and halve the mushrooms.
2 Cut onion into rings and soften in olive oil. Add mushrooms and cook gently for 5 minutes.
3 Season with pepper, salt and crushed garlic.
4 Add lemon juice, white wine and tomato purée.
5 Simmer for 5 minutes.
6 Sprinkle with chopped parsley and leave to cool in the cooking juices.

CHERRY TOMATOES WITH CHEESE AND HERBS
MUSHROOMS A LA GRECQUE
BUTTERNUT SQUASH CHIPS

35

CHEESE DIP

4 oz (100 g) Roquefort
  cheese
1 tbsp (1x15 ml spoon)
  single cream
2-3 tbsps (2-3x15 ml
  spoons) mayonnaise
1 tbsp (1x15 ml spoon)
  lemon juice
lime or lemon peel, grated

1 Make sure the Roquefort is at room
  temperature. Crush into a paste with cream
  and mayonnaise.
2 Add lemon juice.
3 Garnish with grated lime or lemon peel.
4 This dip can be served with various
  vegetables, such as celery, fennel or
  cauliflower.

MULTI-COLOURED DIP

2-3 small gherkins
½ red pepper
1 small onion
3½ fl oz (100 ml)
  mayonnaise
3 tbsps (3x15 ml spoons)
  tomato ketchup
2 tbsps (2x15 ml spoons)
  yoghurt
pepper
salt
pinch paprika

1 Saving some gherkins and pepper for
  garnish, chop gherkins, pepper and onion
  very finely.
2 Mix with mayonnaise, ketchup and
  yoghurt.
3 Season the sauce with pepper, salt and
  paprika.
4 Garnish with bits of gherkin and pepper.

CELERY DIP

2 sticks celery
3½ fl oz (100 ml)
  mayonnaise
2 tbsps (2x15 ml spoons)
  tomato ketchup
1 tbsp (1x15 ml spoon)
  soft white cheese
1 tbsp (1x15 ml) dry
  sherry
Worcestershire sauce
pepper
salt
cayenne pepper

1 Remove the outer fibres from the celery
  and grate the sticks finely. Use the inside
  sticks as they have more flavour.
2 Mix celery with ketchup, cheese, sherry
  and mayonnaise to make a smooth sauce.
3 Season mixture with Worcestershire sauce,
  pepper, salt and cayenne pepper. Use
  celery salt, if possible, instead of salt to
  accentuate the taste of the celery.

DIPS AND SAUCES

CHEESE DIP
MULTI-COLOURED DIP
CELERY DIP

PRAWN SAUCE
APPLE CURRY
HERB MAYONNAISE

GARLIC MAYONNAISE
TUNA DIP
PAPRIKA DIP

2 cloves garlic, crushed
1 egg yolk
pepper
salt
4 tbsps (4x15 ml spoons)
　olive oil
3½ fl oz (100 ml) olive oil
chives and garlic for
　garnish

GARLIC MAYONNAISE

1　Mix egg yolk with garlic.
2　Season with pepper and salt.
3　Stirring continuously, pour in the two sorts of oil to make a thick mayonnaise. Make sure that the egg yolk and oil are kept at room temperature.
4　Garnish with chives and small pieces of garlic.

bunch chives, finely
　chopped
bunch parsley, finely
　chopped
bunch chervil, finely
　chopped
1 egg
1 tbsp (1x15 ml spoon)
　mustard
3½ fl oz (100 ml) olive
　oil
pepper
salt
juice of ½ lemon

HERB MAYONNAISE

1　Separate the egg. Mix egg yolk with mustard in a bowl.
2　Pour oil in a thin trickle into bowl, stirring continuously to make a thick sauce.
3　Season with pepper, salt and lemon juice.
4　Beat the egg white until it is stiff and fold into the mayonnaise to make a very light mixture.
5　Stir in the herbs.
6　Garnish with parsley

½ can or jar of peeled red
　peppers
1 tbsp (1x15 ml spoon)
　wine vinegar
2-3 tbsps (2-3x15 ml
　spoons) yoghurt
salt
pepper
cayenne pepper
2-3 chives

PAPRIKA DIP

1　Drain the peppers and set aside a small amount for garnish. Purée the rest in a blender with the vinegar.
2　Add yoghurt and season with pepper, salt and cayenne pepper.
3　Garnish the dip with strands of chives and small pieces of pepper.

1 small can tuna in oil
2 anchovy fillets
1 tbsp (1x15 ml) capers
3½ fl oz (100 ml)
  mayonnaise
lemon juice
sprig of parsley

TUNA DIP

1 Drain the tuna well, saving some of the oil. Purée tuna with anchovy fillets and capers in a blender, adding a little tuna oil and juice from the capers to give the dip more flavour.
2 Add mayonnaise and season with lemon juice to taste.
3 Garnish with capers and a sprig of parsley.

1 apple
juice of ¼ lemon
1 tsp (1x5 ml spoon) curry
  powder
4 tbsps (4x15 ml spoons)
  mayonnaise
3-4 tbsps (3-4x15 ml
  spoons) yoghurt
pepper
salt
chives, chopped

APPLE CURRY

1 Peel and core apple, cut into quarters and grate very finely.
2 Cover with lemon juice immediately to stop apple going brown.
3 Add curry powder, mayonnaise and yoghurt.
4 Season with salt and pepper.
5 Garnish with chives.

4 oz (100 g) peeled
  prawns
2-3 tbsps (2-3x15 ml
  spoons) milk
3½ fl oz (100 ml)
  mayonnaise
pinch garlic salt
freshly ground pepper
a few drops of Tabasco

PRAWN SAUCE

1 Set aside several prawns for garnish. Purée rest of prawns and milk in a blender. Add mayonnaise.
2 Season with garlic salt, pepper and Tabasco.
3 Garnish with prawns.

SERVING SUGGESTION

Any of these recipes can be used to make this tasty snack.
Cut fingers from slices of white bread and remove the crusts. Spread each finger with a sauce of your choice and roll up like a sausage. Lay the rolls in aluminium foil and leave in the refrigerator until needed.

YOGHURT SAUCE

2 cloves garlic, finely
   chopped
4 shallots, finely chopped
1 green chilli, seeded and
   finely chopped
bunch parsley, finely
   chopped
bunch chives, finely
   chopped
1 tsp (1x5 ml spoon)
   lemon peel, grated
1 lb, 2oz (500 g) natural
   yoghurt
pepper
salt

1 Mix garlic, shallots, chilli and herbs with
   yoghurt.
2 Season with grated lemon peel, pepper and
   salt.
3 Garnish the sauce with pieces of lemon
   peel and chives. This is delicious with raw
   vegetables (crudités) or with artichoke
   leaves which have been cooked and
   cooled.

BAGNA CAUDA

Bagna cauda is a Provencal method of
preparing a sauce for raw vegetables
(crudités). The sauce is kept hot in an
earthenware dish placed over a candle flame.
An ordinary ovenproof dish can be used
instead.

1 can anchovy fillets
2 cloves garlic, crushed
2-3 tbsps (2-3x15 ml
   spoons) single cream

1 Heat the anchovy fillets in their oil in a
   saucepan. Crush to a paste with a fork.
2 Add garlic and cream.
3 Serve with a selection of sliced vegetables.

AVOCADO DIP

juice of ½ lemon
pinch salt
1 avocado
1 clove garlic, chopped
1 bunch coriander
7 fl oz (200 ml) olive oil
ground chilli

1 Dissolve salt in the lemon juice.
2 Peel avocado, cut in half lengthways and
   remove the stone.
3 Dice avocado flesh and purée in a blender
   with lemon juice and garlic.
4 Gradually add oil and coriander leaves.
5 Flavour with ground chilli to taste and
   garnish with sprigs of coriander.
6 Put the avocado stone in the middle to
   prevent dip from changing colour.

BAGNA CAUDA
YOGHURT SAUCE
AVOCADO DIP

43

1 shallot, finely chopped
5 tbsps (5x15 ml spoons)
  sherry vinegar
pepper
salt
5 tbsps (5x15 ml spoons)
  groundnut oil
5 oz (150 g) foie gras
  (goose liver)
2-3 chives, finely chopped

FOIE GRAS VINAIGRETTE

For ten spoons

1 Cook shallot for 1 minute in vinegar seasoned with pepper and salt.
2 Remove from heat and add oil.
3 Keep the sauce hot.
4 Dice the foie gras and cook for 30 seconds without any extra fat in a non-stick frying pan.
5 Put foie gras in spoons.
6 Add chopped chives to the vinegar and pour on to the foie gras.

½ can of peeled red
  peppers
3 tbsps (3x15 ml spoons)
  tomato purée
pepper
salt
cayenne pepper
7 oz (200 g) sardines
1 oz (30 g) butter
sprigs of fresh dill

SARDINE IN PEPPER SAUCE

For ten spoons

1 To make the sauce, purée the peppers, tomato purée, pepper, salt and cayenne pepper in a blender.
2 Gently heat the sauce.
3 Meanwhile, cook sardines in butter for 1 minute.
4 Put sauce into spoons and add a piece of sardine to each.
5 Garnish with a sprig of dill.

¾ oz (20 g) sorrel, finely
  chopped
¾ oz (20 g) spinach,
  finely chopped
pinch parsley, chopped
1 oz (30 g) butter
1 thin eel, skinned
3½ fl oz (100 ml) dry
  white wine
1 egg yolk
lemon juice
parsley for garnish

EEL IN WHITE WINE

For ten spoons

1 Fry the vegetables and parsley in butter until brown.
2 Cut eel into pieces, put on top of vegetables and cover with white wine.
3 Cook for 5-8 minutes.
4 Remove pan from heat and stir in the egg yolk and a little lemon juice.
5 When the eel has cooled, remove the bone and put pieces of eel into spoons with a little sauce.

CANAPES IN A SPOON

FOIE GRAS VINAIGRETTE
SARDINE IN PEPPER SAUCE
EEL IN WHITE WINE

3 tomatoes
1 tbsp (1x15 ml spoon)
  olive oil
10 lettuce leaves
10 peeled prawns
salt
sugar

PRAWNS IN LETTUCE PARCELS

For ten spoons

1 Plunge tomatoes in boiling water for 10 seconds, then peel and remove seeds.
2 Chop the flesh finely and fry for 3 minutes in olive oil. Season with salt.
3 Blanch the lettuce leaves.
4 Wrap prawns in lettuce leaves. Heat the parcels in the tomato sauce, sprinkle with sugar and put parcels and sauce into spoons.

10 small snails
2 cloves garlic, crushed
butter
pastis
½ cup stock
3½ fl oz (100 ml) single
  cream
pepper
salt

SNAILS WITH GARLIC

For ten spoons

1 Fry garlic in butter until brown.
2 Add stock and a dash of pastis.
3 Stir in cream and reduce the mixture.
4 Add the washed snails and season with pepper and salt.
5 Serve snails in spoons with a little sauce.

1 shallot, finely chopped
3 oz (80 g) butter
3½ fl oz (100 ml) dry
  sherry
10 scallops
pepper
salt
1 tsp (1x5 ml spoon) curry
  powder
3½ fl oz (100 ml) single
  cream

SCALLOPS IN CURRY CREAM

For ten spoons

1 Fry shallot in a knob of butter until soft.
2 Add sherry and cook for 2 minutes.
3 Poach scallops in the sherry for 1 minute then remove from pan.
4 Add pepper, salt, cream and curry powder. Reduce the sauce to half.
5 Add the rest of the butter and reheat scallops in sauce.
6 Serve in spoons.

PRAWNS IN LETTUCE PARCELS
SNAILS WITH GARLIC
SCALLOPS IN CURRY CREAM

PASTA WITH GARLIC

20 pasta shapes
salt
1 tbsp (1x15 ml spoon)
    olive oil
1 clove garlic, finely
    chopped
small pinch pili-pili (dried
    chilli seeds)

For ten spoons

1 Cook pasta in boiling salted water.
2 Meanwhile, gently fry garlic and pili-pili in olive oil.
3 Drain the pasta and reheat in the spicy dressing.
4 Arrange the pasta shapes in pairs in the spoons and serve hot.

RAGOUT OF WILD MUSHROOMS

7 oz (200 g) mixed wild
    mushrooms
water
1 oz (30 g) butter
1 clove garlic, crushed
meat extract
pepper
salt
parsley, chopped

For ten spoons

1 Brush mushrooms with water without getting them too wet.
2 Cook mushrooms in butter with garlic and a little meat extract until the juice has completely evaporated.
3 Season with salt and pepper, and put into spoons.
4 Garnish with chopped parsley.

CURRIED CHICKEN

7 oz (200 g) white chicken
    meat
1 apple
1 oz (30 g) butter
3½ fl oz (100 ml) chicken
    stock made from a cube
1 tsp (1x5 ml) curry
    powder
pepper
salt
3 tsps (3x5 ml spoons)
    single cream

For ten spoons

1 Slice chicken thinly.
2 Peel the apple, remove the core and cut the fruit into small dice.
3 Cook chicken and apple together in butter, add curry powder and mix well.
4 Cover with chicken stock and simmer for 5 minutes.
5 Season with pepper and salt.
6 When the sauce has reduced to half, add cream and reduce again.
7 Put the curried chicken in the spoons and serve hot.

PASTA WITH GARLIC
RAGOUT OF WILD MUSHROOMS
CURRIED CHICKEN

7 oz (200 g) filleted brill
juice of ¼ lemon
salt
pepper
9 fl oz (250 ml) carrot
  juice
½ tsp (1x2.5 ml spoon)
  honey
pinch cayenne pepper
1 tsp (1x5 ml spoon)
  cumin

FILLET OF BRILL IN CARROT SAUCE

For ten spoons

1 Cover fish with lemon juice and season with pepper and salt.
2 Meanwhile, heat carrot juice, honey and cumin. Reduce to half.
3 Add cayenne pepper, pepper and salt.
4 Keep sauce hot while you braise the fish.
5 Pour a little sauce into each spoon and add a piece of fish.

10 fresh mussels
3½ fl oz (100 ml) white
  wine
saffron strands
1 clove garlic
3 tbsps (3x15 ml spoons)
  single cream
pepper
fresh dill leaves

MUSSELS IN SAFFRON SAUCE

For ten spoons

1 Clean the mussels thoroughly. Discard any with open shells. Put mussels in a saucepan with white wine, saffron and garlic clove. Cover and cook for 8 minutes or until shells have opened.
2 Strain sauce. Return it to pan and reduce to half. Add cream and reduce to half again.
3 Remove mussels from shells. Keep the sauce hot.
4 Put sauce into spoons and add a mussel to each. Garnish with dill leaves.

2-3 quail's eggs
7 oz (200 g) fillet of beef
oil for frying
salt
pepper
fresh parsley, chopped

BEEF WITH QUAIL'S EGGS

For ten spoons

1 Boil the eggs for 3 minutes. Meanwhile, seal meat by frying quickly in hot oil. Season with salt and pepper.
2 Slice the eggs. Cut beef into 10 pieces.
3 Put the meat into spoons and garnish with a slice of quail's egg and chopped parsley. Serve immediately.

BEEF WITH QUAIL'S EGGS
MUSSELS IN SAFFRON SAUCE
FILLET OF BRILL IN CARROT SAUCE

51

The word 'tapa' literally means 'small lid' and it is thought that the idea of tapas developed from a 19th century Spanish custom when a barman would cover a customer's glass of sherry with a snack such as a slice of ham to prevent the alcohol from evaporating. Today, tapas are made from a variety of different ingredients.

CHORIZO AND SERRANO HAM TAPAS

5 slices chorizo
5 slices Serrano ham
10 small gherkins
5 cocktail onions
5 stuffed olives
1 red pepper

For ten tapas
1 Wrap gherkins in slices of chorizo and Serrano ham.
2 Put on to cocktail sticks.
3 Garnish with pieces of red pepper, cocktail onions and stuffed olives.

HARICOT BEANS VINAIGRETTE

handful large dried haricot beans
salt
freshly ground pepper
3 tbsps (3x15 ml spoons) white wine vinegar
6 tbsps (6x15 ml spoons) olive oil
bunch parsley, finely chopped

For four servings
1 Soak haricot beans in water overnight.
2 Next day, cook them in the same water for 1-2 hours and then drain.
3 Make a vinaigrette with vinegar, oil, pepper and salt to taste.
4 Mix the parsley and beans together.
5 Soak in vinaigrette for at least two hours or until soft.

CAULIFLOWER WITH LEMON AND GARLIC

1 small cauliflower
juice of 1 lemon
1 clove garlic, crushed
4 tbsps (4x15 ml spoons) olive oil
2-3 chives, chopped

For four servings
1 Divide cauliflower into florets and cook or steam.
2 Add lemon juice and garlic when florets are cool.
3 Pour on olive oil and sprinkle with chopped chives.

SPANISH TAPAS

CHORIZO AND SERRANO HAM TAPAS
HARICOT BEANS VINAIGRETTE
CAULIFLOWER WITH LEMON AND GARLIC

11 oz (300 g) small
  calamari
1 clove garlic, finely
  chopped
1 shallot, finely chopped
½ red pepper
½ green pepper
1 carrot
3 tbsps (3x15 ml spoons)
  olive oil
juice of ½ lemon
pepper
salt
6-8 juniper berries

CALAMARI SALAD

For ten servings
1 Clean the calamari.
2 Dry on kitchen paper and cut into strips.
3 Remove seeds from peppers. Cut peppers and carrot into small dice.
4 Cook the calamari in oil without letting them go red and add peppers, carrot, shallot and garlic.
5 Pour lemon juice into the mixture. Cover pan and simmer for 15 minutes.
6 Season with pepper and salt. Add juniper berries.
7 Leave to cool in the cooking juices.

11 oz (300 g) fresh
  anchovy fillets
salt
4 tbsps (4x15 ml spoons)
  olive oil
1 clove garlic, crushed
1 glass white wine
lemon juice
fresh parsley, chopped

MARINATED ANCHOVY FILLETS

For ten servings
1 Salt the anchovy fillets.
2 Simmer in olive oil for 1 hour.
3 Drain, keeping the oil.
4 To the oil, add garlic, wine, a dash of lemon juice and parsley.
5 Simmer for 5 minutes.
6 Pour the marinade on to the fish and leave to soak overnight.

1 lb, 2oz (500 g) calamari
flour
2 eggs, beaten
pepper
salt
oil for frying
1 lemon

FRIED CALAMARI

For four servings
1 Clean the calamari and cut the bodies into rings.
2 Coat in flour.
3 Add salt and pepper to eggs and soak the calamari in the mixture.
4 Fry in oil and serve hot with lemon wedges.

FRIED CALAMARI
MARINATED ANCHOVY FILLETS
CALAMARI SALAD

½ red pepper, diced
½ cucumber, diced
1 clove garlic, chopped
1 tomato
2 tbsps (2x15 ml spoons)
   wine vinegar
1 tbsp (1x15 ml spoon)
   olive oil
18 fl oz (500 ml) water
pepper
salt
cayenne pepper

GASPACHO

For ten bowls
1 Plunge the tomato into boiling water for
   10 seconds, peel and remove seeds.
2 Put all the vegetables with vinegar and oil
   into a blender and make into a thick purée.
3 Add water and season with pepper, salt
   and cayenne pepper.
4 Leave the gaspacho in the refrigerator
   until you are ready to serve it. Serve in
   small bowls.

1 jar green olives, stoned
2 shallots, chopped
1 tbsp (1x15 ml spoon)
   dried oregano
1 clove garlic, crushed
juice of ½ lemon
olive oil
white wine

MARINATED OLIVES

For four servings
1 Drain the olives and mix with shallots,
   garlic, oregano and lemon juice.
2 Put the mixture into a jar and cover with
   equal amounts of olive oil and white wine.
   Seal jar with lid.
3 Leave to marinate in the refrigerator for 24
   hours and serve in a salad.

14 oz (400 g) small
   gambas (prawns)
½ can or jar peeled red
   peppers
2 oz (50 g) ground
   almonds
pepper
salt
2 tbsps (2x15 ml spoons)
   vinegar
2 tbsps (2x15 ml spoons)
   olive oil
2 tbsps (2x15 ml spoons)
   tomato purée

GAMBAS IN
ROMESCU SAUCE

For four servings
1 Cook the gambas by the method described
   on page 98 for Gambas à la plancha.
2 Drain peppers and purée to a smooth sauce
   with almonds, pepper, salt and vinegar.
3 Add olive oil and tomato purée.
4 Serve with the gambas.

GAMBAS IN ROMESCU SAUCE
GASPACHO
MARINATED OLIVES

57

MUSHROOM CANAPES

5 slices toast
9 oz (250 g) mushrooms
¾ oz (20 g) butter
juice of ½ lemon
1 clove garlic, crushed
dry sherry
3½ fl oz (100 ml) single
  cream
pepper
salt

For ten canapés

1 Remove crusts from toast and cut the slices in two.
2 Slice mushrooms and simmer in butter with lemon juice and garlic.
3 Add a dash of sherry and reduce the mixture to half.
4 Add cream and reduce to half again.
5 Season with salt and pepper.
6 Spread the mixture on the toast.
7 Brown under the grill.

HERRING CANAPES

5 slices toast
5 fillets pickled herring
1 oz (30 g) butter
1 oz (30 g) flour
3½ fl oz (100 ml) full
  cream milk
3½ fl oz (100 ml) single
  cream
1 egg yolk
pepper
salt

For ten canapés

1 Remove crusts from toast and cut the slices in two.
2 Put half a herring fillet on to each slice.
3 Make a béchamel sauce: melt butter and stir in flour. Gradually add the milk and then the cream. Bring to boil, stirring all the time.
4 Add egg yolk, salt and pepper.
5 Spoon béchamel sauce on to herrings and brown under the grill.

CHEESE AND BACON CANAPES

5 slices toast
1 large onion, finely
  grated
2 oz (50 g) Gouda cheese,
  grated
2 oz (50 g) bacon, cut into
  thin strips
10 tbsps (10x15 ml
  spoons) mayonnaise
black pepper

For ten canapés

1 Remove crusts from toast and cut the slices in two.
2 Mix onion with cheese, bacon and mayonnaise.
3 Season with pepper to taste.
4 Spread the mixture on to the toast and brown under the grill.

MUSHROOM CANAPES
HERRING CANAPES
CHEESE AND BACON CANAPES

½ baguette
11 oz (300 g) chicken
   livers
1 oz (30 g) butter
1 shallot, chopped
1 tbsp (1x15 ml spoon)
   capers
pepper
salt
1 glass dry marsala
juice of 1 lemon
lemon peel

CROSTINI WITH CHICKEN LIVERS

For ten canapés

1 Cut baguette into 10 thick slices and grill on both sides.
2 Fry shallot in butter, add chicken livers and simmer for 5 minutes.
3 Purée the mixture in a blender with 1 tsp (1x5 ml spoon) capers.
4 Put the liver pâté into a pan with marsala and lemon juice.
5 Reduce to a thick paste which is easy to spread. Season with pepper and salt.
6 Spread paste on to baguette slices and garnish each with pieces of lemon peel and a caper.

½ baguette
1 clove garlic
1 tomato
salt
virgin olive oil

BRUSCHETTA

For ten canapés

1 Cut baguette into 10 thick slices and grill on both sides.
2 Cut clove of garlic and tomato in half. Rub the slices of bread with garlic and tomato.
3 Sprinkle with salt and drizzle with olive oil.

1 red pepper
1 green pepper
oil for coating
1 tbsp (1x15 ml spoon)
   capers
2 anchovy fillets, finely
   chopped
1 clove garlic, crushed
olive oil

MARINATED PEPPERS

For four servings

1 Coat peppers in oil and put them in a hot oven until the skins begin to blacken and come away.
2 Peel, remove seeds and cut into strips.
3 Mix with capers.
4 Add anchovies and garlic.
5 Cover with olive oil and leave to marinate for several hours at room temperature.

ITALIAN ANTIPASTI

MARINATED PEPPERS
BRUSCHETTA
CROSTINI WITH CHICKEN LIVERS

61

GRILLED RADICCHIO
RICE CROQUETTES WITH PARMESAN
FOECACCINE

MARINATED ARTICHOKE HEARTS
CHERRY TOMATOES WITH TUNA
MOZZARELLA IN CARROZZA (TOASTED SANDWICH)

63

1 can artichoke hearts
juice of 1 lemon
4 tbsps (4x15 ml spoons)
   olive oil
bunch fresh basil, finely
   chopped
salt

MARINATED ARTICHOKE HEARTS

For four servings
1 Drain the artichoke hearts and lay them in a small dish.
2 Add lemon juice, olive oil and basil.
3 Season with pepper and salt to taste. Serve chilled.

15 cherry tomatoes
salt
1 small can tuna in oil
1 tbsp (1x15 ml spoon)
   capers with their juice

CHERRY TOMATOES WITH TUNA

For fifteen canapés
1 Cut tops off tomatoes and scoop out the insides.
2 Sprinkle salt in tomatoes and leave upside down to drain.
3 Drain tuna and chop finely.
4 Add capers with a little of their juice.
5 Stuff the tomatoes with the mixture and serve chilled.

10 slices bread
1 Mozzarella cheese
milk
flour
2 eggs, beaten
1 oz (30 g) butter

MOZZARELLA IN CARROZZA (TOASTED SANDWICH)

For five toasted sandwiches
1 Cut the bread into circles the same size as the cheese.
2 Slice Mozzarella and make 5 sandwiches with the bread.
3 Soak each sandwich first in milk, then flour and finally beaten egg.
4 Fry in butter on both sides.
5 Serve hot.

7 oz (200 g) flour
1 tsp (1x5 ml spoon)
  powdered yeast
olive oil
salt
1 onion, sliced into rings

FOECACCINE

For ten rolls

1 Sift flour and salt into a mixing bowl and add yeast and a few drops of olive oil. Add enough water to make an elastic dough.
2 Knead for 10 minutes and leave to rise for 20 minutes.
3 Knead again and leave to rise for another 40 minutes.
4 Make ten balls of dough and flatten them. Coat with olive oil, sprinkle with salt and garnish with onion rings.
5 Cook for 5-8 minutes in an oven preheated to 250°C/480°F or Gas Mark 9.
6 Serve warm.

1 radicchio
olive oil
salt

GRILLED RADICCHIO

For four servings

1 Slice the radicchio lengthways and coat with olive oil.
2 Grill or cook on a barbecue, turning often, until crispy.
3 Sprinkle with salt and serve hot.

9 oz (250 g) rice
¾ oz (20 g) butter
chicken stock made from
  a cube
2 oz (50 g) Parmesan
  cheese, grated
black pepper
1 egg yolk
1 egg, beaten
breadcrumbs
oil for frying

RICE CROQUETTES WITH PARMESAN CHEESE

For fifteen croquettes

1 Cook rice in butter, stirring continuously, and add the chicken stock a little at a time until the rice is cooked and dry (15 minutes).
2 Leave to cool.
3 Add Parmesan, a little black pepper and egg yolk.
4 Shape mixture into balls. Dip balls into beaten egg and then breadcrumbs.
5 Fry in oil and serve hot.

7 oz (200 g) small
  calamari
1 lb, 2 oz (500 g) mussels
9 oz (250 g) clams
2 oz (50 g) peeled prawns
1 shallot, finely chopped
¼ red pepper, thinly sliced
olive oil
lemon juice

SEAFOOD SALAD

For 6-8 servings
1 Clean the calamari, mussels and clams.
   Cut calamari into pieces.
2 Put mussels and clams into a pan with ½
   glass water. Cover and cook until shells
   open.
3 Remove from shells. Cook the calamari in
   the cooking juices from the mussels for 10
   minutes.
4 Mix calamari with mussels, clams and
   prawns.
5 Gently fry shallot and pepper in olive oil.
6 Add to the seafood.
7 Sprinkle with lemon juice and olive oil.

10 large olives, stoned
4 oz (100 g) minced veal
1 clove garlic, crushed
pepper
salt
bunch parsley, chopped
flour
1 egg, beaten
breadcrumbs
oil for frying

FRIED OLIVES

For ten canapés
1 Mix minced veal with the garlic, pepper,
   salt and parsley.
2 Stuff olives with the mixture. Dip olives in
   flour, then in beaten egg, and the
   breadcrumbs.
3 Fry in oil and drain on kitchen paper.
   Serve hot.

4 eggs, hard-boiled
1 small can tuna in oil
pepper
salt
cayenne pepper
2 tbsps (2x15 ml spoons)
  mayonnaise
stuffed olives, sliced

STUFFED EGGS

For eight canapés
1 Peel hard-boiled eggs, cut in two
   lengthways and remove yolks.
2 Chop yolks finely and mix with the
   drained tuna.
3 Season with pepper, salt and cayenne
   pepper.
4 Add mayonnaise and mix to a paste which
   is easy to spread.
5 Stuff the egg halves with the mixture and
   garnish each with a slice of olive.

FRIED OLIVES
SEAFOOD SALAD
STUFFED EGGS

1 ripe cantaloup melon
8 thin slices Parma ham

MELON WITH PARMA HAM

For sixteen canapés
1 Cut melon in two, remove seeds and divide each half into eight. Cut the slices of ham into two lengthways.
2 Peel melon slices and roll each one in a strip of ham.
3 Serve chilled.

7 oz (200 g) semolina
27 fl oz (750 ml) chicken stock
10 slices lean bacon
pepper
salt

BACON POLENTA

For twenty canapés
1 To make the polenta, bring chicken stock to boil and add semolina. Season with pepper and salt and cook gently for 30 minutes.
2 Spread a thick layer of polenta on to a board or worktop, leave to cool and cut into squares.
3 Cut bacon into squares of the same size.
4 Cook bacon for few minutes in a non-stick frying pan.
5 Put bacon on to the squares of polenta and serve immediately.

2 aubergines
salt
2 fl oz (50 ml) olive oil
2 cloves garlic, chopped
black pepper
1 chilli
3 tbsps (3x15 ml spoons) red wine vinegar
1 tbsp (1x15 ml spoon) dried oregano
bunch basil, finely chopped

MARINATED AUBERGINES

For eight servings
1 Cut aubergines lengthways into thin strips.
2 Sprinkle with salt and leave to stand for 45 minutes.
3 Rinse and dry aubergine. Fry on both sides in olive oil.
4 Arrange on a serving dish and sprinkle with garlic, pepper, small pieces of chilli, oregano and basil.
5 Cover with wine vinegar and leave to marinate overnight at room temperature.

MARINATED AUBERGINES
MELON WITH PARMA HAM
BACON POLENTA

7 oz (200 g) dried haricot
  beans
1 clove garlic, chopped
sage leaves
2 tbsps (2x15 ml spoons)
  olive oil
3 tbsps (3x15 ml spoons)
  tomato purée
black pepper
salt

HARICOT BEANS WITH SAGE AND TOMATO

For four servings
1 Soak haricot beans overnight in cold water.
2 The next day, cook in fresh water, adding a sage leaf, for 1½-2 hours.
3 Fry garlic in olive oil, adding a few sage leaves.
4 Add tomato purée and cook gently for 5 minutes.
5 Add beans, salt and pepper.
6 Cook gently for another 5 minutes and leave to cool.

7 oz (200 g) dried haricot
  beans
1 onion, chopped
juice of 1 lemon
1 small can tuna
4 tbsps (4x15 ml spoons)
  olive oil
bunch parsley, chopped
pepper
salt

HARICOT BEANS WITH TUNA

For four servings
1 Soak the haricot beans overnight in cold water.
2 The next day, cook in fresh water for 1½-2 hours.
3 Drain tuna and flake.
4 Mix beans with onion, lemon juice, tuna and olive oil.
5 Garnish with chopped parsley and season with salt and pepper.

7 oz (200 g) dried haricot
  beans
1 onion, chopped
juice of 1 lemon
4 tbsps (4x15 ml spoons)
  olive oil
pepper
salt
7 oz (200 g) chitterling
  sausage
1 tbsp (1x15 ml spoon)
  margarine

HARICOT BEANS WITH CHITTERLING SAUSAGE

For four servings
1 Soak the haricot beans overnight in cold water.
2 The next day, cook in fresh water for 1½-2 hours.
3 Mix beans with onion, lemon juice, olive oil, pepper and salt.
4 Cut the sausage into small pieces, prick and cook in the margarine.
5 Pile the beans on to a plate and garnish with pieces of sausage.

HARICOT BEANS WITH TUNA
HARICOT BEANS WITH CHITTERLING SAUSAGE
HARICOT BEANS WITH SAGE AND TOMATO

1 small fennel
1 courgette
1 broccoli stalk
salt
1 clove garlic, crushed
2 tbsps (2x15 ml spoons)
  wine vinegar
1 small chilli
1 tbsp (1x15 ml spoon)
  capers
green or black olives
4 tbsps (4x15 ml spoons)
  olive oil
pepper
salt

MARINATED VEGETABLES

For 6-8 servings

1 Clean the vegetables. Dice fennel and courgette. Divide broccoli into florets.
2 Blanch vegetables separately in lightly salted water.
3 Drain vegetables and mix with garlic, vinegar, a few rings of chilli, capers, olives and olive oil.
4 Season with pepper and salt and leave to marinate overnight at room temperature before serving.

7 oz (200 g) carpaccio
  (beef fillet)
½ baguette
virgin olive oil
salt
capers

CROSTINI CARPACCIO

For ten canapés

1 Leave the meat in the refrigerator for 1 hour.
2 Slice chilled meat very thinly.
3 Cut baguette into 10 thick slices and grill on both sides.
4 Drizzle with olive oil, sprinkle with salt and cover with slices of beef.
5 Garnish with capers.

5 oz (150 g) black olives,
  stoned
1 tbsp (1x15 ml spoon)
  capers
3 anchovy fillets
2 tbsps (2x15 ml spoons)
  olive oil
½ baguette
sprigs of fresh parsley

CROSTINI WITH ANCHOVY PASTE

For ten canapés

1 Put olives, capers, anchovy fillets and olive oil into a blender and mix to a thick paste which is easy to spread.
2 Cut baguette into 10 thick slices, grill on both sides and spread with anchovy paste.
3 Garnish with parsley.

CROSTINI WITH ANCHOVY PASTE
MARINATED VEGETABLES
CROSTINI CARPACCIO

1 packet fish fritters
oil for frying
5 tbsps (5x15 ml spoons)
  soy sauce
1 tbsp (1x15 ml spoon)
  nuoc mam (spicy fish
  sauce)
2 tbsps (2x15 ml spoons)
  lemon juice
chives

FISH FRITTERS IN PIQUANT SAUCE

For ten canapés
1 Fry fritters in oil and drain on kitchen paper.
2 Serve with a piquant sauce made from soy sauce, nuoc mam and lemon juice.
3 Garnish the sauce with chives.

5 oz (150 g) soya bean
  sprouts
4 oz (100 g) peeled
  prawns, finely chopped
1 small piece ginger,
  finely chopped
dried Chinese mushrooms
1 egg, beaten
filo pastry
oil for frying
lettuce leaves

SPRING ROLLS

For four rolls
1 Drain bean sprouts if necessary.
2 Soak mushrooms in lukewarm water and cut into thin strips.
3 Mix bean sprouts, prawns, ginger and mushrooms with the beaten egg. Divide the mixture between 4 pieces of filo pastry.
4 Roll pastry round mixture to form croquettes and fry in oil.
5 Cut the spring rolls into pieces and arrange on lettuce leaves. Serve with the same piquant sauce as for the fish fritters (see above).

1 red or green pepper
2 tbsps (2x15 ml spoons)
  semolina
11 oz (300 g) mixed
  minced meat
1 egg white, beaten
1 shallot, chopped
1 tbsp (1x15 ml spoon)
  soy sauce
1 tbsp (1x15 ml spoon)
  dry sherry
3 tbsps (3x15 ml spoons)
  sesame oil

STUFFED PEPPERS

For ten canapés
1 Cut pepper in two lengthways, remove seeds and core.
2 Cover insides with semolina.
3 Mix the rest of the semolina with minced meat, egg white, shallot, soy sauce and sherry.
4 Stuff the pepper halves with the mixture and steam for 10 minutes in a pressure cooker.
5 Cut pepper into smaller pieces.
6 Fry the pieces in sesame oil. Serve hot.

ASIAN CANAPES

STUFFED PEPPERS
SPRING ROLLS
FISH FRITTERS IN PIQUANT SAUCE

5 merguez sausages
1 tbsp (1x15 ml spoon)
  ras-al-hanout (spice for
  cous-cous)

MERGUEZ KEBABS

For twenty canapés

1 Cut each merguez sausage in four pieces
  by flattening the mince with your fingers
  and twisting the sausages at equal
  intervals.
2 Stick sausages on to metal skewers or put
  them on to cocktail sticks.
3 Grill and season lightly with ras-al-hanout.
4 Serve hot.

1 packet of falafel mix
bunch coriander, chopped
water
1 green chilli
3 tbsps (3x15 ml spoons)
  olive oil
oil for frying

FALAFEL BALLS

For fifteen canapés

1 Mix the falafel with half the chopped
  coriander and add enough water to make a
  paste.
2 Shape into balls and fry in oil.
3 Clean chilli, and purée in a blender with
  rest of coriander and olive oil to make a
  piquant sauce.
4 Serve the chilli sauce with the hot falafel
  balls.

1 can chick peas
1 clove garlic, crushed
3 tbsps (3x15 ml spoons)
  olive oil
juice of 1 lemon
pepper
salt
pitta bread

HOUMOUS DIP

For four servings

1 Drain chick peas and purée in a blender
  with garlic and olive oil to make a smooth
  paste.
2 Season with lemon juice, pepper and salt.
3 Put the houmous into a bowl and serve
  with triangles of grilled pitta bread.

ARABIAN CANAPES

MERGUEZ KEBABS
FALAFEL BALLS
HOUMOUS DIP

½ cucumber, grated
7 oz (200 g) natural
  yoghurt
1 tbsp (1x15 ml spoon)
  olive oil
1 clove garlic, crushed
salt
parsley, chopped

TZATZIKI

For four servings
1 Mix yoghurt and cucumber.
2 Stir in olive oil. Season with garlic and salt.
3 Serve the tzatziki in small bowls, garnished with a sprinkling of chopped parsley.

2 tbsps (2x15 ml spoons)
  olive oil
1 large onion, finely
  chopped
4 oz (100 g) mixed
  minced meat
4 oz (100 g) rice, boiled
juice of 1 lemon
pepper
salt
16 vine leaves
water

STUFFED VINE LEAVES

For twelve portions
1 Fry onion in a spoonful of olive oil.
2 Add meat, cook and mash well with a fork.
3 Add rice and half the lemon juice. Mix well.
4 Season with pepper and salt.
5 Rinse the vine leaves and stuff them with the mixture.
6 Put any mixture left over in a casserole.
7 Lay the stuffed vine leaves on top, add the rest of the olive oil, lemon juice and a little water and simmer for 30 minutes.
8 Serve cold.

4 oz (100 g) cod's roe
1 potato, cooked
1 shallot, chopped
1 tbsp (1x15 ml spoon)
  olive oil
juice of ½ lemon
15 lemon balm leaves
15 small toast circles

TARAMASALATA TOAST

For fifteen snacks
1 Purée cod's roe, potato, shallot and olive oil to a smooth paste in a blender.
2 Season with lemon juice.
3 Spread the paste on the toasts and garnish each with a leaf of lemon balm.

78

GREEK APPETIZERS

STUFFED VINE LEAVES
TZATZIKI
TARAMASALATA TOAST

1 small piece fresh ginger,
  peeled and grated
10 scampi tails, frozen or
  fresh
3 tbsps (3x15 ml spoons)
  sesame oil
pinch chilli powder
4 tbsps (4x15 ml spoons)
  sesame seeds

SCAMPI WITH SESAME SEEDS

For four servings
1 Put scampi, ginger and sesame oil in a
   wok or pan, mix well and cook until
   scampi turn pink.
2 Cool, then shell scampi.
3 Cook sesame seeds in a non-stick frying
   pan without extra fat.
4 Add scampi and chilli powder. Coat
   scampi with sesame seeds.

½ cucumber
salt
1 piece dried seaweed
  (wakame)
1 tbsp (1x15 ml spoon)
  soy sauce
pinch sugar
1 tbsp (1x15 ml spoon)
  sake (Japanese drink)

CUCUMBER WITH SEAWEED

For four servings
1 Slice cucumber thinly, sprinkle with salt
   and leave to drain.
2 Soak seaweed and cut into thin strips.
3 Add sugar to soy sauce and mix with sake.
4 Press out any remaining moisture from the
   cucumber slices. Mix cucumber with
   seaweed and sauce.

1 lb, 2oz (500 g) spinach
salt
2 tbsps (2x15 ml spoons)
  soy sauce
2 tbsps (2x15 ml spoons)
  mirin (Japanese vinegar)
pinch sugar
1 tbsp (1x15 ml spoon)
  sesame seeds

MARINATED SPINACH

For four servings
1 Wash spinach thoroughly.
2 Holding them by the stalks, soak spinach
   leaves for a few seconds in boiling salted
   water, then in cold water.
3 Remove the stalks.
4 Make a sauce with soy sauce, vinegar and
   sugar. Toss spinach in the sauce.
5 Spoon the spinach on to small dishes and
   garnish with sesame seeds.
6 Serve with French bread.

80

JAPANESE APPETIZERS

CUCUMBER WITH SEAWEED
MARINATED SPINACH
SCAMPI WITH SESAME SEEDS

1 thin slice turkey fillet
1 tbsp (1x15 ml spoon)
  soy sauce
1 tbsp (1x15 ml spoon)
  dry sherry
pinch chilli powder
liquid honey

TURKEY KEBABS

For ten canapés

1 Flatten turkey fillet with the blade of a kitchen knife and cut into thin strips about 2 inches (5 cm) long.
2 Make a marinade with soy sauce, sherry, chilli powder and a little honey. Marinate the strips of turkey for 30 minutes.
3 Roll up turkey and put on to cocktail sticks.
4 Cook for 10 minutes in an oven preheated to 200°C/400°F or Gas Mark 6, turning from time to time.

2 leeks
3 oz (75 g) butter
1 egg, beaten
3 tbsps (3x15 ml spoons)
  flour
milk
pepper
salt
1 tbsp (1x15 ml spoon)
  cumin seeds

LEEK PANCAKES

For ten pancakes

1 Wash leeks thoroughly and cut into small pieces. Simmer in 1 oz (30 g) butter until all the juice has evaporated.
2 Add flour to beaten egg, stir in leeks and add enough milk to make a smooth paste.
3 Season with pepper, salt and cumin.
4 Cook small pancakes in the rest of the butter.
5 Roll up pancakes and secure with cocktail sticks.

1 cauliflower
4 oz (100 g) flour
3½ fl oz (100 ml) beer
1 egg, separated
1 tsp (1x5 ml spoon) oil
oil for frying
salt

FRIED CAULIFLOWER

For 8-10 servings

1 Divide cauliflower into florets.
2 Mix flour with beer, egg yolk and oil.
3 Beat egg white until stiff and add to the mixture.
4 Coat cauliflower florets in the mixture and fry in oil.
5 Drain on kitchen paper and sprinkle with salt.

HOT CANAPES

FRIED CAULIFLOWER
LEEK PANCAKES
TURKEY KEBABS

KIPPER SNACKS
SEAFOOD VOL-AU-VENTS
WHITE PUDDING WITH RED CABBAGE

BLACK PUDDING WITH APPLE COMPOTE
COCKTAIL SAUSAGE ROLLS
CHICKEN LIVERS WITH GINGER

85

1 lb, 2 oz (500 g) mussels
3 ½ fl oz (100 ml) white
  wine
4 oz (100 g) cod fillet
1 oz (30 g) butter
1 oz (30 g) flour
1 tsp (1x5 ml spoon)
  tomato purée
pepper
salt
cayenne pepper
lemon juice
20 small vol-au-vent cases
fresh dill leaves

SEAFOOD
VOL-AU-VENTS

For twenty vol-au-vents
1 Clean mussels thoroughly. Cook them in
  the white wine for 8 minutes.
2 Remove shells and strain juice into a pan.
3 Poach cod in liquor from mussels. Cut cod
  into pieces and save liquor.
4 Melt butter, stir in flour and gradually add
  liquor from fish (stirring all the time) until
  you have a smooth sauce.
5 Flavour sauce with the tomato purée,
  pepper, salt, a little lemon juice and
  cayenne pepper.
6 Reheat mussels and cod in the sauce.
  Meanwhile, heat the vol-au-vent cases in a
  moderate oven.
7 Fill cases with the mixture and garnish
  with sprigs of dill.

2 kippers (smoked
  herring)
cracked peppercorns
rind of 1 lemon

KIPPER SNACKS

For fifteen canapés
1 Cook the kippers on both sides in a
  non-stick frying pan without extra fat.
2 Cut into pieces put on to cocktail sticks.
3 Sprinkle kipper pieces with pepper and
  strips of lemon peel and serve warm.

1 jar of red cabbage with
  apple
1 white pudding
2 oz (50 g) butter
2-3 chives

WHITE PUDDING WITH RED
CABBAGE

For ten canapés
1 Gently heat the red cabbage.
2 Cut white pudding into slices and fry on
  both sides in butter.
3 Put red cabbage and two slices of pudding
  on each plate.
4 Garnish with chives.

1 jar or can stewed apple
ground cinnamon
1 black pudding
2 oz (50 g) butter
bunch chervil

BLACK PUDDING WITH APPLE COMPOTE

For ten canapés

1 Gently heat the stewed apple and season with cinnamon.
2 Cut pudding into slices and fry on both sides in butter.
3 Put stewed apple and two slices of pudding on each plate.
4 Garnish with chervil leaves.

10 pieces frozen puff pastry
20 cocktail sausages
1 egg yolk

COCKTAIL SAUSAGE ROLLS

For twenty sausage rolls

1 Thaw the pastry, lay the pieces out next to each other on a work surface and cut each one in two.
2 Roll a cocktail sausage in each strip of pastry. Seal edges of pastry with water.
3 Put the sausage rolls side by side on a baking sheet.
4 Glaze with egg yolk and bake in a preheated oven at 200°C/400°F or Gas Mark 6 for 15-20 minutes.

7 oz (200 g) chicken livers
1x½-inch (1 cm) piece fresh ginger
2 oz (50 g) butter
1 small glass port
pepper
salt

CHICKEN LIVERS WITH GINGER

For ten canapés

1 Cut chicken livers into pieces and drain on kitchen paper.
2 Peel ginger and cut into slices, then into small strips.
3 Cook chicken liver pieces in butter and add ginger.
4 Add port and reduce liquid by half.
5 Season with pepper and salt and serve hot.

3-4 potatoes
salt
2 oz (50 g) butter
a little milk
pepper
nutmeg
1 shallot, finely chopped
1 clove garlic, crushed
handful mixed herbs,
  chopped
flour
2 egg whites, beaten
breadcrumbs
oil for frying

HERB AND POTATO BALLS

For twenty snacks
1 Peel and boil potatoes.
2 Mash potatoes with butter and a little milk.
3 Season with pepper, salt and nutmeg.
4 Mix in shallot, garlic and herbs.
5 Shape the mixture into balls and dip first in flour, then egg whites and finally breadcrumbs.
6 Fry in oil until brown.

2 lb, 4 oz (1 k) mussels
flour
2 oz (50 g) butter
1 clove garlic, crushed
juice of 1 lemon
pepper
parsley, chopped

FRIED MUSSELS WITH GARLIC

For 6-8 servings
1 Clean mussels. Discard any with open shells.
2 Put mussels and ½ glass water into pan. Cover and cook for a few minutes, until mussels open.
3 Leave to cool, then remove from shells.
4 Coat mussels in flour. Heat butter and add garlic. Brown mussels in hot butter, turning often. Sprinkle with pepper and lemon juice.
5 Garnish with chopped parsley and serve hot.

15 clams
4 oz (100 g) butter
1 tbsp (1x15 ml spoon)
  chervil, chopped
1 tbsp (1x15 ml spoon)
  parsley, chopped
1 clove garlic, finely
  chopped
1 tsp (1x5 ml spoon)
  mustard
pepper
salt
nutmeg

CLAMS IN GARLIC BUTTER

For 6-8 servings
1 Open clam shells with a knife.
2 Lay clams (in half shells) on a thin bed of salt on a baking sheet.
3 Mix butter with herbs, garlic, mustard, pepper, salt and nutmeg.
4 Put a little herb butter on each clam and place under hot grill until butter starts to sizzle.
5 Sprinkle with chopped parsley and serve hot.

HERB AND POTATO BALLS
CLAMS IN GARLIC BUTTER
FRIED MUSSELS WITH GARLIC

89

1 lb (450 g) minced beef
1 egg yolk
1 tsp (1x5 ml spoon)
  mustard
pepper
salt
nutmeg
pili-pili (dried chilli seeds)
2 tbsps (2x15 ml spoons)
  breadcrumbs
chicken stock made from
  a cube
2 tbsps (2x15 ml spoons)
  olive oil
2 shallots, finely chopped
6 tbsps (6x15 ml spoons)
  tomato purée
pinch sugar

MEATBALLS WITH TOMATO SAUCE

For 6-8 servings

1 Mix minced beef with egg yolk, mustard, pepper, salt, nutmeg, pili-pili and breadcrumbs.
2 Shape mixture into balls.
3 Cook for 10 minutes in chicken stock. Meanwhile, fry shallot in oil, add tomato purée and season with salt, pepper and sugar.
4 Drain the meatballs and serve with hot tomato sauce.

1 lb, 2 oz (500 g) fresh
  spinach
salt
1 packet shortcrust pastry,
  rolled out
2 eggs
3½ fl oz (100 ml) cream
pepper
nutmeg

SPINACH TARTLETS

For sixteen tartlets

1 Blanch spinach leaves in boiling salted water.
2 Drain and press to squeeze out excess water.
3 Cut out circles of pastry and line small, greased tartlet tins.
4 Beat eggs with cream and season with pepper, salt and nutmeg.
5 Mix in the spinach. Pour mixture on to pastry.
6 Bake in a preheated oven at 200°C/400°F or Gas Mark 6 for 20 minutes.

10 pieces puff pastry,
  frozen
10 tsps (10x5 ml spoons)
  tomato purée
1 Mozzarella cheese,
  sliced into 10
salt
1 tsp (1x5 ml spoon) dried
  oregano
1 tbsp (1x15 ml spoon)
  olive oil

MINI-PIZZAS

For ten pizzas

1 Thaw pastry, cut out small circles and place on a greased baking sheet.
2 Put a spoonful of tomato purée on each pizza base.
3 Cover with a slice of Mozzarella. Sprinkle with salt and oregano.
4 Sprinkle with a few drops of olive oil and cook in a preheated oven at 250°C/480°F or Gas Mark 9 for 10 minutes.

90

MEATBALLS IN TOMATO SAUCE
SPINACH TARTLETS
MINI-PIZZAS

2 potatoes
1 oz (30 g) Gruyère
  cheese, grated
1 shallot, finely chopped
pinch salt
¾ oz (20 g) butter
2 tbsps (2x15 ml spoons)
  oil

STRAW POTATOES WITH CHEESE

For ten canapés

1 Peel potatoes and grate into thin strips.
2 Mix with cheese, shallot and salt.
3 Heat butter and oil in a non-stick frying pan and add the potato mixture in small heaps.
4 Press down with a fork and brown on both sides.

3 eggs
salt
pepper
4 tbsps (4x15 ml) single
  cream
4 oz (100 g) butter
1 small jar red lumpfish
  roe

SCRAMBLED EGGS WITH LUMPFISH ROE

For ten ramekins

1 Break eggs into a bowl and season with salt and pepper.
2 Whisk in the cream with a fork.
3 Melt half the butter and cook the eggs in it, stirring continuously. Meanwhile, warm 10 ramekins in the oven.
4 Mix the rest of the butter into the scrambled eggs, stirring until it has melted.
5 Put scrambled eggs into the ramekins and garnish with lumpfish roe.

1 butternut squash
flour
1 egg, beaten
breadcrumbs
¾ oz (20 g) butter
2 tbsps (2x15 ml) oil
6 tbsps (6x15 ml spoons)
  tomato purée
pepper
salt
cayenne pepper
pinch sugar

BUTTERNUT SQUASH WITH TOMATO SAUCE

For 6-8 servings

1 Peel squash and remove seeds.
2 Dice the flesh.
3 Coat first in flour, then beaten egg and finally breadcrumbs.
4 Roast squash pieces in butter and oil until crispy. Meanwhile, heat tomato purée, adding pepper, salt, cayenne pepper and sugar.
5 Pour tomato sauce over the roasted squash pieces and serve immediately.

BUTTERNUT SQUASH WITH TOMATO SAUCE
STRAW POTATOES WITH CHEESE
SCRAMBLED EGGS WITH LUMPFISH ROE

93

MUSHROOMS IN GARLIC BUTTER

10 mushrooms
½ lemon
4 oz (100 g) butter
salt
handful parsley, chopped
1 clove garlic
pepper
nutmeg
breadcrumbs

For ten canapés
1 Remove stalks from mushrooms. Rub mushroom caps with the ½ lemon.
2 Mix butter with salt, parsley, garlic, pepper and nutmeg.
3 Fill the mushroom hollows with the mixture and sprinkle with breadcrumbs.
4 Cook under hot grill until butter starts to sizzle.

CHEESE CANAPES

1 oz (30 g) butter
1 oz (30 g) flour
7 fl oz (200 ml) milk
2 oz (50 g) Gruyère cheese, grated
pepper
salt
nutmeg
juice of ½ lemon
1 egg yolk
10 bread circles
oil for frying

For 15 canapés
1 Make a béchamel sauce: melt the butter, stir in the flour and gradually add the milk.
2 Stir in cheese and season with pepper, salt, nutmeg and lemon juice.
3 Remove from heat and stir in egg yolk.
4 Leave to cool.
5 Put a spoonful of cheese sauce on each piece of bread. Fry base of bread in oil.

BROCCOLI TARTLETS

1 packet shortcrust pastry, rolled out
2 stalks broccoli
salt
2 eggs
3½ fl oz (100 ml) single cream
pepper

For sixteen portions
1 Cut out four circles of pastry and line four small, greased tartlet tins.
2 Divide broccoli into florets, wash and blanch for 2 minutes in boiling salted water.
3 Put the broccoli into the tartlets.
4 Beat eggs with cream, pepper and salt.
5 Pour the mixture on to the broccoli. Cook the tartlets in a preheated oven at 200°C/400°F or Gas Mark 6 for 15 minutes. Cut each tartlet into four.

94

CHEESE CANAPES
MUSHROOMS WITH GARLIC BUTTER
BROCCOLI TARTLETS

20 thin rashers smoked
  streaky bacon
20 dates, stoned

BACON WITH DATES

For twenty canapés
1 Roll dates in bacon rashers.
2 Secure each roll with a cocktail stick.
3 Lay side by side on a baking tray and cook in a preheated oven at 180°C/350°F or Gas Mark 4 for 8-10 minutes.
4 Serve hot.

10 chicken drumsticks
2 tbsps (2x15 ml spoons)
  soy sauce.
1 small glass sherry
1 tbsp (1x15 ml spoon)
  chopped ginger
pepper
salt
paprika
sesame seeds

CHICKEN DRUMSTICKS WITH SESAME SEEDS

For four servings
1 Remove any bits of sinew from chicken.
2 Marinate for half an hour in a mixture of soy sauce, sherry, chopped ginger, pepper, salt and paprika.
3 Sprinkle with sesame seeds and grill for 15 minutes, turning frequently.
4 Serve hot.

9 oz (250 g) potatoes
1 small onion, chopped
1 green chilli, chopped
1 tsp (1x5 ml spoon)
  chopped ginger
1 tbsp (1x15 ml spoon)
  lemon juice
salt
pepper
1 egg white, beaten till
  stiff
flour
oil for frying

GINGER CANAPES

For ten canapés
1 Peel potatoes and boil.
2 Mash potatoes with onion, chilli, ginger and lemon juice.
3 Season with salt and pepper.
4 Shape into small balls and coat in egg white and flour.
5 Fry potato balls in oil for a few minutes until well browned.
6 Drain and serve with an aperitif.

CHICKEN DRUMSTICKS WITH SESAME SEEDS
BACON WITH DATES
GINGER CANAPES

2 lb, 4 oz (1 k) mussels, cleaned
1 glass dry white wine
20 small vol-au-vent cases
4 oz (100 g) butter
bunch dill leaves, chopped
bunch chives, chopped
2 oz (50 g) Gruyère cheese, grated

MUSSEL VOL-AU-VENTS

For twenty vol-au-vents

1 Open mussels by cooking them in the wine for 8 minutes.
2 Leave to cool then remove from shells.
3 Fill vol-au-vent cases with mussels.
4 Mix dill and chives with butter.
5 Put a little herb butter in each vol-au-vent case, top with cheese and brown under medium grill for 5 minutes.

---

20 small gambas (prawns), fresh or frozen
2 tbsps (2x15 ml spoons) sea salt
½ glass water

GAMBAS A LA PLANCHA

For six servings

1 Thaw gambas if frozen.
2 Heat a non-stick frying pan and cook gambas a few at a time, sprinkling with sea salt, until they turn red.
3 Pour a little cold water on to each one and allow the excess to evaporate. This makes them very juicy.

---

1 fillet salmon trout
juice ½ lemon
bunch dill leaves, chopped
2 packets puff pastry
curry powder
pepper
salt
1 egg yolk, beaten

SALMON TROUT TURNOVERS

For ten canapés

1 Cover fish with lemon juice and dill. Leave for a while for fish to absorb the flavour.
2 Meanwhile, cut out 20 circles of pastry. Cut the fish into 10 pieces. Put a piece of fish on to a pastry circle.
3 Sprinkle with curry powder, pepper and salt.
4 Cover fish with a circle of pastry. Seal the edges with water.
5 Glaze with egg yolk.
6 Put the turnovers on a greased baking sheet and bake in a preheated oven at 200°C/400°F or Gas Mark 6 for 15 minutes.

MUSSEL VOL-AU-VENTS
SALMON TROUT TURNOVERS
GAMBAS A LA PLANCHA

8 slices bread
2 tbsps (2x15 ml spoons)
  butter
¼ Munster cheese (semi-
  hard)
1 tbsp (1x15 ml spoon)
  mustard
8 thin rashers bacon
melted butter

MUNSTER CHEESE SANDWICHES

For sixteen canapés
1 Mix butter and mustard with cheese and spread on to four slices of bread.
2 Put two rashers of bacon on top of each.
3 Cover each one with another slice of bread.
4 Spread melted butter on the top surface of each sandwich and brown in a preheated oven at 200°C/400°F or Gas Mark 6.
5 Cut the sandwiches into quarters.

20 small circles rye bread
4 round goat's cheeses
dried oregano
olive oil

RYE BREAD WITH GOAT'S CHEESE

For twenty canapés
1 Cut each cheese into five thick slices and put a slice on to each piece of bread.
2 Sprinkle with oregano and a few drops of olive oil.
3 Grill the canapés for 5 minutes until the cheese begins to melt.

8 pieces puff pastry,
  frozen
3 onions
1 oz (30 g) butter
1 tbsp (1x15 ml spoon)
  flour
pepper
salt
nutmeg
7 fl oz (200 ml) cream
2 eggs
4 oz (100 g) Parmesan
  cheese, grated

CHEESE AND ONION TARTLETS

For eight tartlets
1 Thaw the pastry.
2 Grease eight tartlet tins and sprinkle with flour. Line with pastry.
3 Cut onions into thin rings and brown in butter. Sprinkle with flour and brown slightly.
4 Add cream. Sprinkle with salt, and cool.
5 Beat eggs with pepper, salt, nutmeg and Parmesan. Mix with onions.
6 Fill each tartlet with the mixture.
7 Cook in a preheated oven at 200°C/400°F or Gas Mark 6 for 30 minutes.

MUNSTER CHEESE SANDWICHES
RYE BREAD WITH GOAT'S CHEESE
CHEESE AND ONION TARTLETS

101

ARTICHOKE HEARTS WITH HAM

1 can artichoke hearts, drained
1 glass dry white wine
5 oz (150 g) ham
2 oz (50 g) Gruyère cheese, grated
paprika
fresh parsley, chopped

For six servings

1 Braise artichoke hearts in wine for 5 minutes. Meanwhile, dice the ham.
2 Lay artichoke hearts on a baking sheet, stuff them with ham and top with grated cheese.
3 Season with paprika and grill for 5 minutes. Garnish with chopped parsley.

MINCEMEAT SNACKS

2 eggs
2 cloves garlic, crushed
2 tbsps (2x15 ml spoons) mustard
pepper
salt
bunch parsley, chopped
3 tbsps (3x15 ml spoons) breadcrumbs
1 lb, 11 oz (750 g) mixed minced meat
4 carrots, grated
stuffed olives, sliced

For twenty canapés

1 Mix meat with eggs, crushed garlic, mustard, pepper, salt, parsley and breadcrumbs. Press mixture together firmly.
2 Lay out in a thin layer on a baking sheet. Cook in a preheated oven at 180°C/350°F or Gas Mark 4 for 20-25 minutes.
3 Cut the meat mixture into squares and garnish with grated carrot and slices of olive.

MINI-BURGERS WITH QUAIL'S EGGS

14 oz (400 g) minced lamb
pepper
salt
fresh thyme, chopped
fresh rosemary, chopped
7 oz (200 g) margarine
20 fresh quail's eggs
cayenne pepper

For 20 mini-burgers

1 Season the minced lamb with pepper, salt, thyme and rosemary. Wet your hands and shape meat into 20 balls. Fry quickly in some hot margarine.
2 Melt the remaining margarine in a non-stick frying pan and sprinkle with salt. Break the quail's eggs into the pan and fry.
3 Remove the white and top each burger with a fried yolk.
4 Season with cayenne pepper.

ARTICHOKE HEARTS WITH HAM
MINCEMEAT SNACKS
MINI-BURGERS WITH QUAIL'S EGGS

FRENCH BREAD WITH GRAPES

1 baguette
2 cloves garlic
3½ fl oz (100 ml) olive oil
bunch white grapes

For 6-8 people
1 Cut baguette in half lengthways and then cut each half into pieces.
2 Crush garlic. Put in a bowl and add oil.
3 Beat the oil mixture.
4 Brush oil mixture on to the crusts.
5 Garnish the bread with small pieces of grape.

PEAR SLICES WITH GORGONZOLA

5 canned pears
4 oz (100 g) Gorgonzola, finely grated
4 oz (100 g) cream cheese
capers

For ten canapés
1 Drain pears and cut in half lengthways.
2 Make sure the cheeses are at room temperature. Mix Gorgonzola with cream cheese and put the mixture into a piping bag.
3 Pipe a rosette on to each piece of pear and garnish with a caper.

BANANA FRITTERS

2 bananas
4 oz (100 g) flour
3½ fl oz (100 ml) beer
1 egg, beaten
1 tsp (1x5 ml spoon) olive oil
oil for frying

For twelve fritters
1 Peel bananas, cut in two lengthways and then cut each half into three pieces.
2 Mix flour, beer, beaten egg and olive oil thoroughly to make a smooth paste.
3 Coat the banana pieces in the paste and fry in oil.

FRUIT CANAPES

FRENCH BREAD WITH GRAPES
PEAR SLICES WITH GORGONZOLA
BANANA FRITTERS

APPLE CANAPES

2 crisp apples
2 oz (50 g) butter
3 oz (80 g) caster sugar
1 liqueur glass calvados
10 mini pastry cases
fresh mint leaves

For ten canapés
1 Wash, peel and core the apples. Cut into dice.
2 Heat butter in a pan and, when it starts to brown, add the diced apple.
3 Sprinkle with sugar, and brown, stirring all the time.
4 Add calvados and flame the mixture.
5 Put diced apple and sauce in the pastry cases. Garnish with a little fresh mint and serve warm.

PEACHES WITH CRAB

1 can crabmeat
cayenne pepper
2 fresh peaches
10 mini pastry cases
½ red pepper

For ten canapés
1 Drain the crab well and divide into small pieces. Season with plenty of cayenne pepper.
2 Dip peaches in boiling water for 10 seconds, peel and dice.
3 Mix the diced peaches with crabmeat and put into the pastry cases.
4 Decorate with small pieces of red pepper.

MANGO AND SCAMPI CANAPES

5-6 scampi tails, shelled
¾ oz (20 g) butter
juice of ½ lemon
1 ripe mango
curry powder
10 mini pastry cases
lime or lemon peel

For ten canapés
1 Cook scampi in butter and lemon juice.
2 Peel mango, remove stone and dice.
3 Season with curry powder.
4 Cut scampi into pieces and put into mini pastry cases with mango.
5 Decorate with small pieces of lime or lemon peel.

MANGO AND SCAMPI CANAPES
APPLE CANAPES
PEACHES WITH CRAB

107

DATES STUFFED WITH CHEESE
PIQUANT PINEAPPLE
APRICOTS WITH COCONUT

108

MELON BALLS WITH PORT
APPLE AND GRAPE CANAPES
STUFFED FIGS

1 ripe pineapple
4 tomatoes
pinch sugar
pepper
salt
1 piece ginger (½ inch/
  1 cm long), finely
  chopped
pili-pili (dried chilli seeds)
pinch curry powder

PIQUANT PINEAPPLE

For eight servings

1 Dip tomatoes in boiling water for 10
  seconds. Peel and remove seeds.
2 Chop tomato flesh into small pieces and
  purée in a blender. Mix with sugar, pepper,
  salt, pili-pili and ginger.
3 Put the sauce in the refrigerator and leave
  for several hours.
4 Meanwhile, cut pineapple into four (or
  into eight) lengthways. Remove the core
  and separate the flesh from the peel.
5 Cut the pineapple in pieces widthways.
  Arrange so that alternate pieces are on the
  left or the right (see photograph page 108).
6 Cover with tomato sauce or serve the
  sauce separately.

20 semi-dried apricots
4 oz (100 g) fresh Brie
4 oz (100 g) full fat cream
  cheese
2 tbsps (2x15 ml spoons)
  grated coconut
20 cranberries

APRICOTS WITH COCONUT

For twenty canapés

1 Flatten apricots and lay side by side on a
  worktop.
2 Mix Brie and cream cheese until smooth.
3 Put the mixture in a piping bag and pipe a
  rosette on to each apricot.
4 Sprinkle with grated coconut and decorate
  with cranberries.

10 dates
3 tbsps (3x15 ml spoons)
  cheese spread
10 half walnuts

DATES STUFFED WITH CHEESE

For ten canapés

1 Cut dates in two lengthways. Remove
  stone.
2 Fill with cheese and put a half walnut on
  each.
3 Serve in small paper cases.

2 cantaloup melons
red port
sprigs of mint

MELON BALLS WITH PORT

For ten canapés

1 Cut melons in half and remove seeds.
2 Use a melon baller to scoop out small balls of fruit and put them into glass dishes.
3 Pour a little port into each dish. Serve chilled.
4 Garnish with sprigs of mint.

3 apples
lemon juice
7 oz (200 g) full fat cream cheese
pepper
salt
1 tbsp (1x15 ml spoons) grated horseradish
5 black grapes, halved and seeded
sprigs of mint

APPLE AND GRAPE CANAPES

For ten canapés

1 Slice apples vertically into 10 circles, stopping before you reach the core.
2 Cover immediately with lemon juice to prevent apple flesh turning brown.
3 Season cheese with pepper and salt. Stir in the grated horseradish.
4 Put the mixture into a piping bag and pipe a rosette on to each slice of apple.
5 Decorate with half a black grape.
6 Stick a sprig of fresh mint into the cheese and chill before serving.

5 fresh figs
1 carton cream cheese
pepper
salt
cress

STUFFED FIGS

For ten canapés

1 Cut figs in half lengthways and put the halves on a serving plate.
2 Season cheese with pepper and salt, and put into a piping bag.
3 Pipe rosettes on to the figs and garnish with cress.

1 honeydew melon
1 cantaloup melon
1 chilli, chopped

SPICED MELON BALLS

For ten servings
1 Cut melons in half and remove seeds.
2 Use a melon baller to scoop out small balls of the fruit. Make sure that the halves are well scooped out.
3 Season melon balls with chilli and put in the refrigerator for 1 hour to absorb the flavour.
4 Put a melon ball of each type on to a cocktail stick. Place the half melon skins upside down on a plate and stick canapés into them.

bunch black grapes
1 egg white
1 sachet vanilla sugar
crushed ice

GRAPES IN SUGAR

For 4-6 servings
1 Separate the bunch of grapes into small groups.
2 Beat egg white until stiff and stir in sugar. Cover grapes, one by one, in egg mixture. Put grapes in the refrigerator for 15 minutes until the sugar crystallises.
3 Serve on crushed ice.

20 strawberries
2 bars fondant chocolate
3 tbsps (3x15 ml spoons) single cream

STRAWBERRIES IN CHOCOLATE

For twenty canapés
1 Break chocolate into pieces and melt by putting into a small saucepan in a pan of boiling water.
2 Stir in cream to make a smooth paste.
3 Dip half of each strawberry into the chocolate sauce and leave upside down until the chocolate has hardened.
4 Serve in small paper cases. Instead of serving the strawberries ready to eat, you can serve the chocolate sauce separately, keeping it warm on a hotplate. Guests dip the strawberries into the sauce themselves.

SPICED MELON BALLS
GRAPES IN SUGAR
STRAWBERRIES IN CHOCOLATE

INDEX

TOAST CANAPES

VEGETABLE CANAPES

DIPS AND SAUCES

CANAPES IN A SPOON

SPANISH TAPAS

ITALIAN ANTIPASTI

ASIAN CANAPES

ARABIAN CANAPES

GREEK APPETIZERS

JAPANESE APPETIZERS

HOT CANAPES

FRUIT CANAPES

© 1992 by Invader Ltd., Chichester PO20 7EQ,
England. All rights reserved.
Original edition: © 1990 by ZNU n.v., Belgium.